P9-CMR-193

CRISISPOINTS FOR WOMEN

GETTING A
GRIP ON GUILT

JUDITH COUCHMAN

NAVPRESS

A MINISTRY OF THE NAVIGATORS
P.O. BOX 6000, COLORADO SPRINGS, COLORADO 80934

248.34

The Navigators is an international Christian organization. Jesus Christ gave His followers the Great Commission to go and make disciples (Matthew 28:19). The aim of The Navigators is to help fulfill that commission by multiplying laborers for Christ in every nation.

NavPress is the publishing ministry of The Navigators. NavPress publications are tools to help Christians grow. Although publications alone cannot make disciples or change lives, they can help believers learn biblical discipleship, and apply what they learn to their lives and ministries.

© 1990 The Navigators
All rights reserved, including translation
ISBN 08910-93249

Cover illustration by David Groff.

CRISISPOINTS FOR WOMEN series edited by Judith Couchman.

This series offers God's hope and healing for life's challenges.

Unless otherwise noted, Scripture quotations in this publication are from the *Holy Bible: New International Version* (NIV). Copyright © 1973, 1978, 1984, International Bible Society. Used by permission of Zondervan Bible Publishers. Another version used is the *New American Standard Bible* (NASB), © The Lockman Foundation 1960, 1962, 1963, 1968, 1971, 1972, 1973, 1975, 1977.

Printed in the United States of America

FOR A FREE CATALOG OF
NAVPRESS BOOKS & BIBLE STUDIES,
CALL TOLL FREE 1-800-366-7788 (USA)
or 1-416-499-4615 (CANADA)

C O N T E N T S

For Nancy L.,
my lifetime friend who knows me well
and loves me anyway.

ACKNOWLEDGMENTS

These endearing and enduring women deserve thanks and recognition:

Opal Couchman for giving unconditional love and encouragement.

Mae Lammers, Madalene Harris, Charette Barta, and Lucy Henderson for proving that proximity has nothing to do with faithfulness in prayer.

Claudia Stafford, for typing countless revisions and still claiming she loves to work for me.

The editors at *Aglow* for first allowing me to explore this topic in their magazine. ∎

When Guilt Won't Go Away

*Why you'll want to use this
study guide.*

On a sunny day in Chicago, a solemn-looking
man stood stiffly on a busy downtown street
corner. As people hurried past him, he slowly
lifted his arm, pointed to an unsuspecting
pedestrian, and yelled, "Guilty!"

Then without any expression, the man
returned to his stiff stance. That is, until he
raised his arm again and screamed "Guilty!"
at another startled person.

The atmosphere turned almost eerie.
Each time the man yelled his judgment,
people stared at him, hesitated, and looked
away. Or they looked at each other and then
hurried down the sidewalk as if they'd been
exposed. One passerby even turned to a
stranger and asked, "How did *he* know?" [1]

Guilt. It's an old, familiar feeling. So
familiar that, for many women, it's a way of
life. Mired in worry and low self-esteem, they

7

can't discern what's true guilt and what's not. No matter how hard they try, these women can't push beyond their guilt to God's love and forgiveness. And it stunts their emotional and spiritual growth.

If you—or women you know—struggle with guilt and an inability to feel forgiven, this study booklet's for you. Alone or with a group, it can help you explore the freedom of forgiveness.

First, read the article, "Am I Really Forgiven?" It's about a time when I struggled with nagging guilt and how I developed a purging point to free myself from it. While a purging point isn't the only way to grapple with guilt, it could help you develop a workable system for facing your sins.

After the article, four lessons will explore why God wants you to get a grip on true and false guilt—and how to find lasting forgiveness.

You can use this study guide in many ways. While it's best to read and study the entire booklet, you may want to ponder just the opening article. Or you might complete only the Bible lessons. Whatever you decide, consider using this guide for:

- Sunday school classes.

- Small-group Bible studies.

- Introducing women to Christ.

- One-on-one study or discipling.

8

• Personal study or devotional times.

• Professional or coffee-cup counseling.

However you use it, remember this study isn't an instant cure-all for a difficult problem. Rather, it will grasp your hand and guide you—or women you know—into the cleansing waters of God's forgiveness. ■
—JUDITH COUCHMAN

NOTE
1. Karl Menninger, M.D., *Whatever Became of Sin?* (New York: E. P. Dutton, 1973), pages 1-2.

Am I Really Forgiven?

A purging point can wash away guilt.

While my car's windshield wipers furiously whapped at the sputtering rain, I glanced skyward and protested: *Oh, no, it can't rain. Not today; not now! Doesn't God realize how important these next few hours are?*

I pressed the gas pedal harder, daring the wipers and an aging engine to clear the road ahead. And for the next half hour we purposefully—almost defiantly—pulsed together: the wipers, the engine, the raindrops, my heart.

Muttering to their rhythm, I repeated my resolve: *I have to get to the ocean. I have to get to the ocean!* Because if I got there, somehow everything would be all right.

Finally at a beach, I quieted the car, rolled up my collar, and stepped into the drizzle. Then while squishing along the

11

shoreline, I pondered what I'd soon dump
into the gray waters.

DUMPING IT OUT

About everything had gone wrong that year.
And I'd topped it all off with a fit of cranki-
ness—downright rudeness—toward my
mother when she visited me at Christmas
time. Poor Mom, always so loving and understanding. I'd really unloaded on her, and my
unhappiness wasn't her fault.

Now she'd gone home, and I stumbled
into the new year with a bundle of remorse.
To me, surliness toward Mom symbolized my
sins and failures of that whole, horrible year.
And no matter how hard I prayed, I couldn't
cast off the accumulated guilt.

So driving to the ocean was my last
shot at absolution—from the way I'd treated
my mother, from my piled-up failures, from
my inability to forgive myself. For some
unexplainable reason, I felt compelled to
return to the seaside spot where I'd sniped at
Mom the worst—and where water, a symbol
of cleansing, flowed freely.

Pulling my coat closer, I mentally culled
out nagging sins and disappointments, one
by one. After I repented and asked God for
forgiveness—or after I forgave someone
else—I imagined dumping each offense into
the sea.

Then I whispered toward heaven, "Lord,
I know Your love and forgiveness runs deeper
and wider than this ocean. So today I've

12

repented, and now I'm accepting Your absolution, once and for all. I'm throwing away this guilt, too!"

The next day my spirit lightened. And for weeks after, I recalled the "big dump" when I felt tempted to relive offenses I'd discarded. *No, you can't pester me,* I'd mentally say to lingering accusations. *I threw my guilt into the ocean on that rainy Sunday.*

Soon even the temptation to feel guilty washed away, lost in the many waters of forgiveness.

A PURGING POINT

From time to time, each in our own way, we reach those waterless places where an inability to accept forgiveness strangles the soul. We feel parched, stymied, haunted. And the customary paths to absolution don't free us from a spiritual desert of shameful feelings. We desire a heart purged of self-pity and doubt. We long for God's reassuring touch.

In essence, we need a purging point—a repentant act that frees us from the sin, the guilt, and the unforgiveness with absolute finality. This act plumbs the depth of our sin and flushes it out, then guards against evil attempts to pollute our confidence in God's mercy. It helps us know we're rock-bottom forgiven, once and for all.

But if we want this forgiveness, we can't wait passively for God to douse us with cleansing waves. We must actively pursue it. We can create a purging point that assures

13

us of forgiveness, whether or not we feel it. It involves repenting, forgiving, memorial building, and standing firm.

DIVING INTO REPENTANCE

Much of our inability to experience forgiveness originates when we feel sorry for our mistakes instead of repentant for our sin. Sorriness only bobs on the surface of wrongdoing; repentance dives to the bottom of sin and eradicates it.

Saying "I'm sorry" just admits getting caught; it doesn't force us to topple pride and view our spiritual wreckage. Saying "I repent" and "Please forgive me" acknowledges our sin and expresses a desire to turn from it. Sorriness evokes emotion. Repentance, though often tearful, willfully decides to change.

We can express repentance with a method that's meaningful to us: alone or with a trusted friend; in our words or with a liturgy; in our heart or with our lips. It's the end result that matters: a clear-cut confession of our iniquity before God and the humble request that He forgive us.

At certain times, we may need to confess offenses accumulated over the years: those we've never confessed; those we've recently recognized as sin; those we've confessed but still feel guilty about; those we've confessed but keep repeating. This could require an extended time of prayer and confession, and this often reaps spiritual renewal.

For example, while serving as a pastor, Richard Foster desired more power in his spiritual walk. So he devised a plan of thorough repentance by dividing his life into three periods: childhood, adolescence, adulthood. After a prayer for God's guidance, he wrote down anything from these periods that needed forgiveness or healing or both.

Paper in hand, Richard then met with a Christian friend and read the list aloud. When he finished reading, he began to place the list in his briefcase, but his friend intercepted the paper, shred it to bits, and dropped them into a wastebasket. He then prayed for the healing of the hurts in Richard's past. And Richard knew, with absolute certainty, that God forgave him.[1]

FORGIVING OUR DEBTORS

There are times, however, when repentance doesn't immediately usher us into cleansing streams. Quite often, we must grant forgiveness before accepting it. The Lord Jesus taught us to pray, "Forgive us our debts, as we also have forgiven our debtors" (Matthew 6:12). Getting and granting forgiveness is a hand-in-glove arrangement.

So if others have wronged us, we need to forgive them—sometimes face to face; other times, just before God. As with repentance, this step demands a willful decision more than an emotional upheaval. It varies with circumstances and personalities.

In his book *Forgiveness,* Charles Stanley

offers guidelines for forgiving others, especially when it's difficult to do so. He suggests:

1. Select a time to be alone. Then ask God to bring to mind all the people you need to forgive.

2. Make a list of everybody—and everything they did—that comes to mind, even if it seems trivial.

3. Arrange two chairs, facing each other. Sit in one of the chairs.

4. Imagine the first person sitting in the other chair. Name everything that person did.

5. Willfully choose to forgive the person forever by saying, "You are free and forgiven."

6. Thank God for using this person to deepen an understanding of His grace. By faith, receive God's unconditional love and acceptance.[2]

GRABBING AT GRACE

Once we've pardoned others, forgiveness doesn't finish there. It's equally important to forgive ourselves. This is probably the hardest step, especially for women. Because of low self-esteem, family background, sensitivity, or deep emotional wounds, we often

can't forgive ourselves. We repeatedly flog
ourselves to prove true repentance, when in
reality, we're exposing an inability to grab
God's grace.

The apostle Peter exhibited self-forgiveness. He "went outside and wept bit-
terly" after denying Jesus Christ three
times to protect himself (Matthew 26:75;
see verses 69-74). Then when Jesus forgave him and said, "Feed my lambs" (John
21:15), Peter rallied into a great spiritual
leader.

At some point, Peter must have forgiven
himself. He believed and fulfilled the proph-
ecy that he'd become the rock on which
Christ would build the church (Matthew
16:18). After Christ's ascension, Peter per-
formed miracles and stood stalwart through
persecution. But he couldn't have wielded
such spiritual power while wallowing in
unforgiveness.

Self-forgiveness needs exercise in many
areas. It's necessary for absolving everyday
mistakes, such as arguing with the boss,
yelling at the kids, or gossiping about a
friend. It's also required for life-changing
failures—ignoring God's call, marrying the
wrong man, or choosing a sinful lifestyle.
If we truly repent, God will forgive any sin
we've committed. So why shouldn't we forgive
ourselves?

The beloved author Catherine Marshall
set a self-forgiving example we can follow.
After her husband Peter died, Catherine
remained single for several years. She

grew lonely and a bit self-pitying. It wasn't because there weren't suitors in her life; it's just that none of them became her second husband.

Along the way, she met Jim, a man who befriended her young son, Peter Junior. Jim lived in Wyoming, but often visited Catherine's hometown on business. Before long, Jim desired companionship with Peter Junior's mother, too. Unhappily married, he longed to divorce his wife and marry Catherine.

Catherine loved Jim's company; she cared about him. She considered his proposition flattering, tempting—and dreadfully wrong. Despite her feelings for Jim, Catherine knew God wouldn't honor a relationship with a married man.

During one of Jim's visits, Catherine arranged for them to visit her pastor, Gordon. He talked to the couple about sin and commitment, and Jim and Catherine agreed, before God and Gordon, to sever their relationship.

They punctuated their agreement with confession, communion, and Gordon's benediction: "Go your separate ways—freely forgiven, restored, refreshed, into new usefulness and creativity." [3]

As evidenced by their lives, Jim and Catherine forgave themselves. Several months later Jim reunited with his wife. Catherine proceeded with a powerful writing ministry that reached millions. And later, she entered a happy second marriage.

Like Jim and Catherine, we can build a memorial to the sacred acts of repentance and forgiveness. So in later moments, months, or years, we can recall our absolution.

Memorial building isn't a new idea. God knows we need assurances of His mercy. He's created symbolic reminders for us, like the rainbow and the cross (Genesis 9:15-16, Colossians 1:19-22). And at specific junctures in history, God has asked people to build memorials according to His instructions.

When Joshua led the Israelites across the Jordan River into the promised land, God wanted His people to remember they'd crossed on dry ground. As they walked between parted waters, one man from each tribe hoisted a stone from the riverbed and carried it to the Canaan bank. They fashioned the twelve stones into a memorial and piled another dozen in the riverbed where priests had shouldered the ark of the covenant.

"Let this be a sign among you," instructed Joshua. "Because the waters of the Jordan were cut off before the ark of the covenant of the LORD. . . . So these stones shall become a memorial to the sons of Israel forever" (Joshua 4:6-7, NASB).

Those stones didn't represent an actual act of absolution, but they symbolized passing from an old life into a new one. And that's the purpose of building a memorial to forgiveness. It reminds us that we've passed from guilt to absolution, from doubt to confidence in God's grace.

A memorial can be as unique as our situation, as creative as imagination. It can be as simple as a phone call noted in a journal, as elaborate as a litany for reconciliation. It can be private or public, planned or spontaneous, physical or imaginary. But always, a memorial is symbolic of the sin we've repented, the forgiveness we've granted, the guilt we've cast off.

STANDING ON STONES

On days when I squirm about my failures that dreadful year, I remember a jar of sea shells sitting on my kitchen counter. I collected the shells after pitching my sins into the ocean, and they remind me that God forgave and forgot those iniquities.

Building a memorial to forgiveness requires a resolve to stand firmly on our heap of stones when the winds of false accusation—from Satan, from others, from ourselves—threaten to topple us. When we doubt our forgiveness, when old habits nibble at us, when resentfulness creeps up again, we can recall the stake-in-the-ground event and remember our cleansing.

With this reminder, we can rebuke Satan and believe in our absolution. Or if we need forgiveness again (and many times we do), the memorial can remind us that God's grace remains available and plentiful.

That happened to Sandy. Trapped by a cold heart, she felt hopeless about ever feeling repentant—let alone forgiven—for past sins. Then one night Sandy pulled out an old journal she'd kept while studying the Bible. Turning the pages, her eyes fell on a list titled "My Sins."

After the list, in a too-familiar scrawl, appeared this confession: *If I had a dollar for each of my big or small defections from the Lord, I'd be a rich woman! Thank You, God, for the softening of my heart. Teach me Your faithfulness. Cleanse me from sin.*

Suddenly Sandy realized she'd traveled this path before—and that God had forgiven her. Reading her confession from three years before renewed Sandy's belief that she could repent, receive forgiveness, and discard her sin again. It also granted her the courage to fight Satan while renewing her spiritual journey.

FLINGING DROPLETS

A purging point can ease pain, break down built-up sin, erase disappointment, mend relationships, release negative emotions, or renew a spiritual commitment. It stands as a memorial to God's forgiveness and, if kept in sight, as a shield against repeating the same offenses.

But it's not a cure-all for those who need prolonged ministry or deep inner healing. In these cases, it can only function as one part of the recovery process. For many of us, though, a purging point can help kick away our sin and guilt.

Yet no matter how symbolic or creative, a purging point renders ineffective if we don't embrace God's mercy. Mother Angelica, a nun who manages a Christian television network, learned this simple truth.

While standing by the sea, a wave splashed the contemplative sister. As she recovered, she thought the Lord asked, "Angelica, do you see the drop on your finger?"

"Yes."

"It represents your sin. Do you also see the vast ocean?"

"Yes, I see that too, Lord."

"The ocean represents My mercy. If you fling the droplet into the sea, could you find it again?"

"No."

"The same is true for your droplet of sin and My ocean of mercy. You can keep your offenses and stay miserable or you can lose them in My mercy. What will you do?"

Angelica flung the droplet into the sea.[4]

So can we. ∎

NOTES

1. Richard Foster, *Celebration of Discipline* (San Francisco, CA: Harper & Row, 1978), pages 130-131.
2. Charles Stanley, *Forgiveness* (Nashville, TN: Oliver-Nelson, 1987), pages 195-196.
3. Catherine Marshall, *Meeting God at Every Turn* (Old Tappan, NJ: Chosen, 1980), page 154.
4. Bert Ghezzi, *Transforming Problems* (Ann Arbor, MI: Servant, 1986), page 32.

An Inside Look

What are you feeling guilty about?

On the following pages, you'll study sin, guilt, grace, and forgiveness. But it won't mean much if the information just stays in your head and doesn't change how you live.

To help apply this material to life—to experience the freedom of God's grace and forgiveness—you first need an inside look at yourself. You need to honestly admit what you feel guilty about; why you've reached a crisispoint; how you'd like God's Word to change you. It's also wise to realize that without God's power you probably can't change much.

So before you begin, get alone to ponder the following questions. Even if you're studying with a group, you can keep the answers confidential. And, of course, don't let these questions make you feel guilty! Simply use them as a private, nonjudgmental

way to open your heart to God, to ask for
His help.

YOUR REASONS

1. Why do you want to study guilt and
   forgiveness?

2. Jot down what you'd like to learn about
   each of these topics.

   Sin:

   Guilt:

Grace:

Forgiveness:

YOUR FEELINGS

3. What things make you constantly feel guilty? Why?

4. What can't you forgive yourself for? Why?

5. Who would confidentially pray for and support you while you're facing the issues in questions 3 and 4? Enlist that person before you start the lessons.

6. In addition to this study, what other resources might help you?

7. Through this study and other resources, how do you want God to change you?

8. a. What disciplines will you need so God can change you?

b. How will you pursue these disciplines?

YOUR PROMISE

9. Ask God to show you a Bible verse to claim as His promise for your forgiveness. (A concordance could help you find a verse.) Write it below, and review it before each lesson.

10. Write a prayer, asking God for insights as you complete this study. ∎

Getting a Grip on Guilt

Are your feelings true or false?

Michelle: *Since the kids entered high school, I've gone back to the work force as a teacher. It feels good to pursue the field I studied for in college, but I feel guilty. I worry about neglecting my family.*

Lorna: *Before I became a Christian and married my husband, I had an abortion. Even though I've asked God to forgive me over and over again, I still feel depressed and guilty.*

Janice: *I'm involved in so many extra-curricular activities, I feel exhausted and irritable. Still, all of the activities are good—church, community, neighborhood stuff. I'd feel guilty dropping out of them.*

Each of these women struggles with guilt.
And though the problems differ, their feelings sound similar. They're battling the
timeless, accusing emotions that point and
cry, "You messed up!" They know guilt's a
nagger.

Guilt doesn't discriminate, either. No
matter the person, no matter the offense,
it can nag, nag, nag. Even if the accusations prove false, guilt can make us miserable. It relentlessly wants our attention.

When we struggle with guilt, it's helpful
to first get a grip on our feelings—to face the
emotions that plague us.

1. Create a metaphor about guilt. A metaphor describes something this way:
   "_____ is like
   _____." For example,
   "Guilt is like living in a garbage can."
   Or "Guilt is like pots and pans banging
   inside my head."
      Write your metaphor. Then list the
   emotions that accompany guilt.

   Metaphor:

Emotions:

GUILT PRODUCERS

Feeling guilty feels awful. But feeling awful doesn't always mean we're really guilty. Once we've pinpointed our feelings, it's important to discern between true and false guilt. True guilt results from sin. False guilt emerges from wrong expectations or untrue accusations, from ourselves or from others.

2. Who can make us feel guilty? Read the verses that follow and pinpoint the guilt producers and the methods they used. Describe each guilt producer's role or relationship to the accused person.

GUILT PRODUCER	METHOD
Psalm 41:5-6	

GUILT PRODUCER	METHOD
Psalm 41:9	
Matthew 20:8-12	
Mark 2:23-24	
Luke 10:38-40	

3. Do any of the above people represent guilt producers in your life? Place a check by them. Can you add yourself to the list? Explain.

4. In the spiritual realm, who can make us feel guilty? How?

GUILT PRODUCER	METHOD
John 8:44, Revelation 12:10	
John 16:7-11	

5. Compare the guilt producers in questions 2 and 4. Next to each item, jot a few words that indicate each person's motivation for making us feel guilty.

Sorting true guilt from false guilt pivots on understanding the guilt producer's motivations. True guilt originates from sin and leads us to confession and restitution. True guilt helps us end the agony.

False guilt stems from people foisting their sin (greed, self-pity, selfishness, etc.) or expectations on us. It also grows from unrealistic expectations for ourselves. False guilt creates never-ending misery.

In her book *Falling Apart or Coming Together,* Lois Walfrid Johnson charts the following differences between true and false guilt.[1]

	TRUE GUILT	FALSE GUILT
GUILT PRODUCER	The Holy Spirit convicts, based on truth.	Satan condemns, based on lies.
OBJECTIVE	Improvement.	Defeat.
SPOTLIGHT	Specific, unforgiven sin.	Past failures and forgiven sin; general in nature.
YOUR REACTION	Remorse and repentance; asking for forgiveness.	Helplessness; a no-win situation; not knowing how to make a change; no peace if you ask for forgiveness.
GUILT PRODUCER'S ACTION	Grace; forgiveness.	Accusation.

	TRUE GUILT	FALSE GUILT
RESULT	Peace; feeling set free, cleansed and loved.	No peace; defeat; hopelessness; despair; worthlessness. Feeling emotionally, spiritually and physically tired.

6. Now describe the false guilt that people inflict on you. Often this guilt creates the feelings, "I should have . . ." or "I didn't . . ." or "I never . . . ." In other words, this false guilt focuses on things you have or haven't done—things that make you try to please people.

Objective:

Spotlights:

Your reaction:

Their action:

Result:

7. Read John 8:44 again, and 1 Peter 5:8.

    a. How does Satan want to place false
       guilt on us?

    b. How can the false guilt from Satan
       and from people be similar in its
       effects on us?

GOD'S HELP

8. When people place false guilt on us, what
   can we remember about our relationship
   with God?

   Psalm 56:11

Romans 8:1-2

Romans 8:38-39

9. How can the directives in the following
   verses help us fight false guilt?

   Matthew 5:44

   Matthew 18:19-20

   Acts 5:29

Philippians 4:8

1 Peter 5:6-7

1 Peter 5:8-10

1 John 1:9

FACE IT

10. Read the list of things you feel guilty about in "An Inside Look" on page 25. In the following chart, list the things that may be false guilt and why they nag you. Then, according to the Scriptures you've studied, decide how to put away your false guilt.

FALSE GUILT	WHY IT NAGS ME	WHAT I CAN DO

FIGHT IT

This week, with your support person, review
how you can attack false guilt (see question
10). Then develop a plan for overcoming
at least one false-guilt feeling. Pray about
the plan and discuss it together each week,
checking your progress. When the false guilt
leaves, celebrate its demise. ∎

NOTE
  1. Lois Walfrid Johnson, *Falling Apart or Coming Together*
     (Minneapolis, MN: Augsburg, 1984), page 66.

When the Guilt's for Real

A look at the nature of sin.

> *The very word "sin," which seems to have
> disappeared, was a proud word. It was
> once a strong word, an ominous and
> serious word. It described a central point
> in every civilized human being's life plan
> and life style.*
>
> *But the word went away. It has
> almost disappeared—the word, along
> with the notion. Why? Doesn't anyone sin
> anymore? Doesn't anyone believe in sin?*[1]
> —Karl Menninger

In the early 1970s, a world-famous psychiatrist startled America with these questions in his book *Whatever Became of Sin?* The doctor warned that sin is alive and well in the world, even though many people felt it had become passé.

But to God, sin never left the heart

of humanity. Neither did the true guilt it produces.

SINFUL OFFENSES

Webster's dictionary defines sin as "an offense against God." [2] In the Old Testament, the word translated as *sin* (*hātā* in Hebrew) means "missing the mark" or standard that God set for humanity. In the New Testament, the word *sin* (*adikia* in Greek) translates to "wrongdoing," "unrighteousness," or "injustice." [3]

1. According to these verses, what causes an offense against God?

   1 Samuel 12:15

   Psalm 95:8-10

   Isaiah 53:6

2. Based on the above verses, what would you say is the root cause of sin?

3. In one sentence, write a simple definition of sin.

SERIOUS DESCRIPTIONS

4. In the Bible, what are some adjectives (descriptive words) used to describe sin?

Proverbs 14:34

Proverbs 15:9

Proverbs 30:12

Isaiah 1:18

Hebrews 3:13

5. Read Isaiah 1:4-6 and 30:1. Then describe the seriousness of sin to God.

6. Now write a descriptive definition of sin that offends the senses. What does sin look, feel, taste, and smell like to God?

TEN COMMANDMENTS

If sin offends God, what specific actions are sin? God gave us His eternal moral laws in the Ten Commandments.

7. Read Romans 7:7. Why did God give us the Ten Commandments?

8. Read Exodus 20:3-17. In the chart
   below, briefly state each of God's com-
   mands. Then list some ways each of
   these commandments are violated today.
   A newspaper or magazine could yield
   specific examples.

COMMANDMENTS	VIOLATIONS

INTERNAL VIOLATIONS

Many people say they haven't broken God's
commandments because they think of sin
only in external terms. For example, most of
us haven't murdered anyone.

But Jesus Christ taught that breaking the commandments internally is equivalent to violating them externally.

9. Read Matthew 5:21-22,27-30. How could each of the Ten Commandments be broken inwardly through words, thoughts, or attitudes?

EXTERNAL COMMAND	INTERNAL VIOLATION

10. Read and consider James 2:8-11. What further insights do these verses reveal about breaking the commandments?

TRACING BACK

It's been said that every sin is rooted in one of God's commandments. And every commandment exposes rebellion against God.

11. Read each passage that follows and list the specific sins it names. Then determine the commandment(s) that each sin violates, either externally or internally.

SIN	COMMANDMENT
Proverbs 6:16-19	

SIN	COMMANDMENT
Matthew 15:18-19	
Ephesians 4:29-31	
James 4:17	

12. Read Matthew 22:37-40, in which Christ quotes two additional commandments from the Old Testament.

a. What are the two greatest commandments?

b. Christ said that all of God's law hangs
on these two commandments. What
could He have meant by this?

TRUE GUILT

If we're truly honest, it's impossible to study
God's commandments without recognizing
ways we've broken them externally and
internally. And that's true even if we're
sincere believers in Christ.

13. Where does sin originate?

Psalm 51:5

Matthew 15:18-19

Romans 5:12-14 (Genesis 3)

James 1:13-15

14. Read Romans 3:9-12,23. What do these verses reveal about guiltiness before God?

15. Summarize what this lesson has taught you about sin and humanity's guilt before God.

16. Read the list of commandments in questions 8 and 11. Now personalize what you've learned in this lesson.

a. Circle the number that best represents your response to the following statements, when "1" = never and "5" = always.

I take seriously God's offense with sin.	1	2	3	4	5
I break the Ten Commandments.	1	2	3	4	5
I acknowledge the sin in my life.	1	2	3	4	5
I know when my guilt results from sin.	1	2	3	4	5
I confess my sin daily.	1	2	3	4	5

b. Would you like to change your response to any of the above? If so, how?

This week study the section "Why the Offense?" on pages 79-85. It will help you understand God's holiness and why sin offends Him. ■

NOTES
1. Karl Menninger, *Whatever Became of Sin?* (New York: E. P. Dutton, 1973), pages 1-2.
2. David B. Guralink, ed., *Webster's New World Dictionary* (New York: Simon and Schuster, 1982), page 1328.
3. Lawrence O. Richards, *Expository Dictionary of Bible Words* (Grand Rapids, MI: Zondervan, 1985), pages 566-567.

Grabbing at Grace

Facing the results of true guilt.

*In communion with the living God . . .
the sense of guilt, so far from being
blunted, is sharpened rather. Its depth
and inescapability are revealed still
more.*

    *It is through such humiliation,
through such a conviction of sin, that
access is granted to a personal relationship with God, which is the true solution
to guilt.*[1]   —Paul Tournier

Yes, sin is alive and thriving among us.
But many of us don't want to admit it. We'll
attribute our offenses to many causes—dis-
ease, accident, addiction, independence—anything except the real, root problem of sin.

    Yet the truth is this: We often *feel* guilty
because we *are* guilty. Sin produces true
guilt. And God wants to free us from both.

1. What causes us to feel guilty about sin?

   Psalm 51:3

   Psalm 97:10

   Proverbs 18:19

   John 16:7-8, 1 Corinthians 3:16

   1 Timothy 1:18-19

2. What can keep us from feeling guilty about sin?

   Proverbs 29:1

Romans 1:28-32

Romans 2:5-6

3. Read Romans 1:18-20, 2:12-15. Is igno-
   rance of God's laws an excuse for denying
   sin or guiltiness before God? Explain.

4. According to Romans 6:23, what are
   the consequences for those who refuse
   to accept Christ and His atonement
   for sin?

5. As Christians, what happens when we don't acknowledge our sin to God?

Psalm 66:18

Proverbs 28:13

Romans 6:16

1 John 1:8

6. How might we deny our sin? (What names do we call offenses instead of using the word *sin*?)

7. How did these people deny their guilt before God? What were the results?

DENIAL	RESULTS
Nation of Israel (2 Kings 17:14-20)	
Religious Leaders (Luke 11:39-51)	
Ananias and Sapphira (Acts 5:1-11)	

8. What should be our relationship to sin?

Psalm 19:13

Psalm 32:5

Romans 6:6-7,12

Hebrews 12:1

9. How did these people acknowledge sin before God? What were the results?

ACKNOWLEDGMENT	RESULTS
Prophet Ezra (Ezra 9:1-9, 10:1)	

ACKNOWLEDGMENT	RESULTS
City of Nineveh (Jonah 3:4-10)	
Criminal on the Cross (Luke 23:39-43)	

10. Have you behaved like the people in
    questions 7 or 9? Give specific examples
    by completing the following sentences.

    A time I denied my sin was . . .

The results of denial were . . .

A time I acknowledged my sin was . . .

The results of confession were . . .

11. What may be causing you to deny your sin before God?

GOD'S FEELINGS

12. What are God's actions or feelings toward those who don't confess their sin?

Psalm 7:9-14

Matthew 23:37-38

Mark 3:5

13. What are God's feelings about forgiving
    people of their sin?

    Psalm 103:8-10

    Luke 7:36-50

    2 Peter 3:9

14. What are the results of acknowledging
    and confessing sin?

    Psalm 103:12

    Romans 5:1

Romans 6:22

1 John 1:9

15. Read James 4:6. What can keep us from responding to God's grace?

16. Are you willing to face unconfessed sin in your life? Explain.

This week, review your list of things that make you feel guilty, paying attention to the personal sin. (See page 25.) Add any additional sin to the list.

Then prayerfully answer these questions:

- Why is each of these offenses a sin?

- Why do I persist in this sin?[2]

- Why have I not confessed this sin to God?

- What will make me willing to repent of this sin?

- What will be the results of my confession?

- What will happen if I don't confess this sin? ∎

NOTES
1. Paul Tournier, *Guilt & Grace* (San Francisco: Harper & Row, 1983), page 167.
2. Another CRISISPOINTS study, *So What If You've Failed?*, confronts the problem of besetting sin.

Dumping It Out

Confess, repent, and be forgiven.

God cannot do our repenting for us. In our efforts to magnify grace we have so preached the truth as to convey the impression that repentance is a work of God. This is a grave mistake, and one which is taking a frightening toll on Christians everywhere.

God has commanded all [people] to repent. It is a work which only they can do. It is morally impossible for one person to repent for another. Even Christ could not do this. He could die for us, but he cannot do our repenting for us.[1]

—A. W. Tozer

SPECIFIC CONFESSION

If we are willing to confess our sin to God, He is ready to hear and to forgive us.

In the New Testament, the word translated *confess* (*homologeō*) from the Greek language means "acknowledge." Drawing from the legal system of that time, "to confess" meant the accused would agree with the charge brought against them and acknowledge their guilt before the court. So to "confess our sin" means to agree with God that our actions are sinful.

True confession according to the Bible does not just say "I'm sorry." It involves specifically naming the offense and calling it sin.[2]

1. How should we approach the confession of sin?

   Psalm 38:18

   Jeremiah 3:25

   James 4:8-10

2. In Psalm 51, King David acknowledged his sin to God after committing adultery and murder (2 Samuel 11).

   a. Read the entire psalm, then note how David appealed to God in the following verses.

   Verse 1:

   Verse 3:

   Verse 4:

   Verse 7:

Verse 10:

b. In 2 Samuel 12, the prophet Nathan specifically named David's sin, and David agreed with him. Even with a prayer such as Psalm 51, why would it still be important to specifically name the sin we've committed?

3. Summarize how David's example could help you confess sin to God. While following his example, how could you specifically name the sin you've committed?

4. a. How does God prompt us to confess
   our sin?

   John 16:7-8

   Romans 2:4

   Hebrews 4:12-13

   b. How can other people play a role in
   prompting us to acknowledge and confess sin?

   2 Samuel 12:1-9,13

Hebrews 3:13

James 5:16

c. How can you prompt yourself toward confession?

d. Of the options in a, b, and c, how would you most like to be prompted toward confession? What hinders you from this?

The confession of sin is closely aligned with repentance. In the Old Testament, *repent* (*nāhaam*) means "to regret" or "to turn from a previous way." The New Testament word (*metanoia*) reinforces this meaning by emphasizing a "change of mind and attitude." [3]

Confessing sin is part of true repentance, but not all of it. To genuinely repent is to have a "change of mind" about the sin after confessing it. It is deciding to make the changes necessary to discard the sin rather than to entertain and repeat it.

5. Read Acts 26:12-20, in which Paul describes his conversion experience. Also see Christ's words in Luke 13:1-5. How does our eternal salvation pivot on repentance?

6. After accepting Christ as Savior, how does repentance allow us to fellowship with God? See Hebrews 10:19-23.

7. Read Isaiah 29:13-14. What can we substitute for true repentance?

8. a. How can we tell if genuine repentance has occurred?

Joel 2:12-13a

Matthew 3:8

Luke 19:1-9

2 Corinthians 7:9-10

b. What other indicators of true repentance can you add to the above?

REAL FORGIVENESS

Once we confess and repent, God does not insist that we keep groveling before Him. He longs to forgive us and forget the offense.

9. a. What do these verses reveal about God's attitude toward confessed sin?

   Isaiah 38:17

   Jeremiah 31:34b

Micah 7:18-19

b. What is your response to these
   descriptions of God's forgiveness?

10. What could hinder God from hearing our
    prayer of confession?

    Matthew 5:23-24

    James 4:2-3

11. How should God's forgiveness toward us
    affect our relationship with others?

Luke 6:36-38

Romans 2:1-3

TRUE FAITH

12. According to Ephesians 2:8-9 and
    Hebrews 11:6, what is necessary on our
    part to receive forgiveness?

13. Read Ephesians 6:10-18. How can we
    keep the devil from stealing the faith
    that we're given?

Understanding God's forgiveness is not enough. We must take action to receive it. In review, that action includes:

- **Confession:** specifically naming the offense and agreeing with God that it is sin. The Ten Commandments can serve as a guideline for identifying sin.

- **Petition:** asking God to forgive the sin we've confessed to Him.

- **Repentance:** choosing to change in a way that forsakes the sin.

- **Reconciliation:** asking for forgiveness or absolving others of their sin against us.

- **Acceptance:** believing that God has truly forgiven us.

- **Abandonment:** following God's example and forgetting the offense.

14. Based on Proverbs 8:32-36, how often should we confess sin?

15. Think of a sin you need to acknowledge before God. How can you follow each of these steps toward forgiveness? Specifically state what you can say or do.

Confession:

Petition:

Repentance:

Reconciliation:

Acceptance:

Abandonment:

Using the above steps as a guideline, confess the sin to God. You may want to use this list to create a purging point as described on pages 13-14 and 87-88. Date and sign this page to document your confession and forgiveness.

You can use these steps to confess additional or future sins.

Signature:

Date:

LOOKING AHEAD

This week, develop a plan for making confession part of your daily life. Ask your prayer partner to hold you accountable for the plan. ■

NOTES
1. A.W. Tozer, *Paths to Power* (Harrisburg, PA: Christian Publications, Inc., n.d.), pages 17-18.
2. Lawrence O. Richards, *Expository Dictionary of Bible Words* (Grand Rapids, MI: Zondervan Publishing, 1985) page 183.
3. Richards, page 522.

Why the Offense?

Understanding God's holiness.

To better understand God's holiness in relationship to sin, read this excerpt from *The
Pursuit of Holiness* by Jerry Bridges and
answer the questions that follow it.

GOD'S HOLINESS

*God is often called in Scripture by such names
as the Holy One, or the Holy One of Israel.
Holy . . . is used more often as a prefix to His
name than any other attribute. Holiness is
God's crown. . . . Holiness is the perfection
of all His other attributes: His power is holy
power, His mercy is holy mercy, His wisdom is
holy wisdom. It is His holiness more than any
attribute that makes Him worthy of our praise.*

*But God demands more than that we
acknowledge His holiness. He says to us, "Be
holy, because I am holy" [1 Peter 1:15-16].*

*God rightfully demands perfect holiness
in all of His moral creatures. It cannot
be otherwise. He cannot possibly ignore or
approve of any evil committed.*[1]

GOD'S HATRED

*Because God is holy, He hates sin. Hate is
such a strong word we dislike using it. We
reprove our children for saying they hate
someone. Yet when it comes to God's attitude
toward sin, only a strong word such as hate
conveys an adequate depth of meaning. . . .*

*We often say, "God hates the sin but
loves the sinner." This is blessedly true, but
too often we quickly rush over the first half of
this statement to get to the second. We cannot
escape the fact that God hates our sins. We
may trifle with our sins or excuse them, but
God hates them.*

*Therefore every time we sin, we are doing
something God hates. He hates our lustful
thoughts, our pride and jealousy, our outbursts
of temper, and our rationalization that the
end justifies the means. We need to be gripped
by the fact that God hates all these things. We
become so accustomed to our sins we sometimes
lapse into a state of peaceful coexistence with
them, but God never ceases to hate them.*

*We need to cultivate in our own hearts
the same hatred of sin God has. Hatred of sin
as sin, not just as something disquieting or
defeating to ourselves, but as displeasing to
God, lies at the root of all true holiness. We
must cultivate the attitude of Joseph, who*

said when he was tempted, *"How then could I do this great evil, and sin against God?"* (Genesis 39:9).

God hates sin wherever He finds it, in saint and sinner alike. He does not hate sin in one person and overlook it in another. He judges each man's works impartially (1 Peter 1:17). . . .

In the deceitfulness of our hearts, we sometimes play with temptation by entertaining the thought that we can always confess and later ask forgiveness. Such thinking is exceedingly dangerous. God's judgment is without partiality. He never overlooks our sin. He never decides not to bother, since the sin is only a small one. No, God hates sin intensely whenever and wherever He finds it.

Frequent contemplation on the holiness of God and His consequent hatred of sin is a strong deterrent against trifling with sin. We are told to live our lives on earth as strangers in reverence and fear (1 Peter 1:17). Granted, the love of God to us through Jesus Christ should be our primary motivation to holiness. But a motivation prompted by God's hatred of sin and His consequent judgment on it is no less biblical.[2]

CROWNING ATTRIBUTE

According to Jerry Bridges, "Attributes as applied to God refer to His essential qualities, and are inferred from Scriptures describing God." [3]

1. Bridges cites the following verses as examples of God's "crowning attribute." Below, write the names given to God that express this attribute.[4]

   Psalm 89:18

   Isaiah 40:25

   Habakkuk 3:3

2. Bridges also cites verses as references to God's holiness. Briefly record what each verse says about the Holy God.

   Exodus 15:11

   Leviticus 19:2

   Psalm 89:35

3. According to Ezekiel 39:7 and Habakkuk 1:13, why is it impossible for God to condone sin?

4. Read Isaiah 6:1-7, in which the prophet Isaiah sees God.

   a. What was the prophet's response to God?

   b. What was God's response to Isaiah?

   c. From what you've learned about sin, do you think Isaiah's response affected God's action? Explain.

5. How can we cultivate a proper response to God's holiness?

Psalm 119:104

Psalm 138:2

Isaiah 57:15

HOLY LIVING

6. How can we be holy (righteous) in God's eyes, even though we're sinners?

Romans 3:21-26

Romans 5:6-8,18-21

Colossians 3:9-12a

7. How should our lives be affected by God's holiness?

   Hebrews 12:14

   1 Peter 1:15-16

8. Does your response to God's holiness need to change? Explain. ∎

NOTES

1. Jerry Bridges, *The Pursuit of Holiness* (Colorado Springs, CO: NavPress, 1978), page 29.
2. Bridges, pages 32-33.
3. Bridges, pages 34-35.
4. Bridges, page 35.

A Purging Point to Call Your Own

Get rid of nagging guilt forever.

You can create your own purging point: a repentant act that frees you from guilt and unforgiveness with absolute finality.

While a purging point can be pursued in many ways, these step-by-step suggestions may help you create your own.

1. Specifically name the guilt that's nagging you. Write it out on paper: in a few words or in detail—whatever suits your needs.

2. Also list the people you want to forgive and why you need to absolve them. If necessary, include yourself.

3. Using a concordance, locate and study verses about God's forgiveness. Claim them for yourself.

4. Plan a purging point activity that will be meaningful to you. Be sure that it meets with the following:

   - Create it to fit your personality and circumstances.
   - Make it symbolic of the sin and guilt you're casting off.

- It should be simple enough to complete in a reasonable amount of time.
- Be sure it can be easily remembered in years to come.

5. Incorporate your list of sins and people into the purging point. Name and confess the sins or forgive the people, one by one. Be specific. Don't ask for or grant a general absolution. Follow the guidelines for forgiveness on page 16.

6. If appropriate, involve a witness, either to watch or to participate. Be sure it's someone you can trust implicitly.

7. Use a symbolic act and words from Scripture to represent God's forgiveness of your sins and your forgiveness of others.

8. Document your confession and forgiveness. Check off the items on your list and write the date next to them. Or create an informal certificate that acknowledges your confession and repentance. Ask your witness to sign the document, too.

9. Celebrate your forgiveness with your witness or someone else you love through an activity you enjoy. Create a memorial to your forgiveness.

10. Place the documentation of your forgiveness in a place where you can easily refer to it. When doubts confront you, review the document and the fact that you are freely, utterly forgiven. ∎

Getting Together About Guilt

Questions for your small group.

LESSON ONE

1. How can we mistake false guilt for true guilt?
2. Why is it important to discern between true and false guilt?
3. Why do we allow people to place false guilt on us? Why do we inflict it on ourselves?
4. Which do we usually focus on most: true or false guilt? Why?
5. Can false guilt ever become an excuse for not facing true guilt? Explain.
6. What effects does false guilt have on us?
7. Are women more prone to false guilt than men? Explain.
8. Why does Satan inflict us with false guilt? How might he do this?
9. Why is false guilt so prevalent today?

10. Who usually places the most false guilt on us? Why?
11. Why is it difficult to eradicate false guilt?

LESSON TWO

1. Why do people feel that the notion of sin is outdated?
2. Are these feelings about sin peculiar to our times? Explain.
3. Why would God choose these particular Ten Commandments?
4. How would you prove to someone that sin exists?
5. Even when we believe in sin, how can we overlook its seriousness?
6. Do most Christians take sin seriously enough? Explain.
7. How can we tell if someone takes sin seriously?
8. If needed, can we begin to take sin more seriously?
9. Can we focus too much on sin? Explain.
10. Can we ever mistake something for sin when it's not? Explain.

LESSON THREE

1. What causes "floating anxiety" or a constant, vague sense of guilt? How is this true of false guilt?
2. Do we need to feel bad to know that we are guilty of sin? Explain.
3. Why is it still possible to sin after becoming a Christian?

4. How does society deny sin and attribute it to other causes?
5. How do we deny sin personally?
6. How do we develop denial in our lives?
7. Is it easier to deny sin than to confess it? Explain.
8. Is denial related to most sin? Explain.
9. What clouds our vision of God's grace?
10. What are the signs of someone who walks in the freedom of God's forgiveness?
11. What are the attitudes of someone who does not confess sin?
12. What is the difference between accepting the remission of sin to become God's child and the confession of sin after becoming a Christian?

LESSON FOUR

1. Why do we need to specifically name our sin before God?
2. How can we ensure that we specifically confess sin?
3. Is it possible to confess sin but not repent of it? Explain.
4. Can we confess sin and not mean it? Explain.
5. Why can it be difficult to confess sin?
6. If we repeat a confessed sin, did we truly repent of it? Explain.
7. Is repentance a one-time action or an ongoing process? In what ways?
8. Why can it be difficult to believe in God's forgiveness?

9. How can we strengthen our faith in God's forgiveness?
10. In what ways can we practice forgetfulness toward forgiven sin?
11. How can we believe God's forgiveness when the consequences of our sin badger us?
12. What can we do to keep from committing sin in the first place? ■

BIBLIOGRAPHY

Toward Guilt-Free Living

*Books for further thought
and study.*

Bridges, Jerry. *The Pursuit of Holiness.*
Colorado Springs, CO: NavPress, 1978.

Mains, Karen. *The Key to a Loving Heart.*
Elgin, IL: David C. Cook Publishing, 1979.

Marshall, Catherine. *Meeting God at Every
Turn.* Old Tappan, NJ: Chosen Books,
1980.

Menninger, Karl. *Whatever Became of Sin?*
New York: Bantam Books, 1984.

Smeades, Lewis B. *Forgive & Forget.* New
York: Pocket Books, 1984.

Stanley, Charles. *Forgiveness.* Nashville, TN:
Oliver-Nelson Books, 1987.

Stokes, Penelope J. *Grace Under Pressure* Colorado Springs, CO: NavPress, 1989.

Thatcher, Martha. *The Freedom of Obedience.* Colorado Springs, CO: NavPress, 1986.

Tournier, Paul. *Guilt & Grace.* San Francisco, CA: Harper & Row, Publishers, 1983.

Tozer, A. W. *Man: The Dwelling Place of God.* Harrisburg, PA: Christian Publications, 1966. ■

A U T H O R

Judith Couchman is Director of Communications for The Navigators. She also serves as a part-time editor for NavPress.

As a freelance writer, Judith has published over 250 manuscripts. She is the former editor of *Sunday Digest* and associate editor of *Christian Life* and has worked as a public relations professional and a journalism teacher. She has also taught writing at conferences around the United States.

Judith has received top awards from the Evangelical Press Association, the International Association of Business Communicators, and several high school press associations.

She holds a B.S. in education from the University of Nebraska at Omaha and an M.A. in journalism from Northern Illinois University. She lives in Colorado Springs, Colorado. ■

OTHER TITLES IN THIS SERIES

Additional *CRISISPOINTS* Bible studies include:

> *Nobody's Perfect, So Why Do I Try to Be?* by Nancy Groom. Get over the need to do everything right.

> *So What If You've Failed?* by Penelope J. Stokes. Use your mistakes to become a more loving, godly woman.

> *When You Can't Get Along* by Gloria Chisholm. How to resolve conflict according to the Bible.

> *You're Better Than You Think!* by Madalene Harris. How to overcome shame and develop a healthy self-image.

> *When Your Marriage Disappoints You* by Janet Chester Bly. Hope and help for improving your marriage.

These studies can be purchased at a Christian bookstore. Or order a catalog from NavPress, Customer Services, P. O. Box 6000, Colorado Springs, CO 80934. Or call 1-800-366-7788 for information. ∎